WORDSNACKS

D1565093

ALSO BY NATASHA METZLER

Pain Redeemed
The Thing About Dairy Farmers

WORDSNACKS

bite-sized devotionals
for your hungry moments

Natasha Metzler

ISBN: 1502821443
ISBN-13: 978-1502821447

Cover photograph © Crew Labs Inc./Glen Carrie

TO NORMA ZEHR

Because she kept asking me when she could
get my devotionals in print. This first edition is for her.

ACKNOWLEDGEMENTS

Everything I know was influenced by someone else.
So thank you to all who have spoken truth into my life.
Thank you to all who have prayed understanding into my heart.
Thank you to each and every Believer who has touched my life in some way.
This book could not exist without your faithfulness.

SEEDS PLANTED

on unplowed ground

WILL NEVER PRODUCE
A HARVEST.

PLOWS AND SEEDS AND BROKENNESS

WordSnack: Psalms 85:1-13

It is so still outside. The pond water runs green and soft. Bull frogs sing refrains that blend with the crickets' symphony and echo across the flat land.

The plow dug furrows this week. Deep, dark, black earth turned skyward. Sod busted up and the remnants of green left to turn brown. Roots torn and dragged, beaten and broken.

In the upturned dirt, tiny pieces of corn will be planted. Sun will shine. Rain will fall. Seeds will break open, all that is dead will fall away and life will triumph, again.

It's so hard when the plow hits the soil of our hearts. Pieces of life are used to work the ground of our souls—tearing, dragging, exposing our darkness, leaving us for dead. It's easy to get caught up in the pain part. To fail to set our gaze on the future glory.

Here's a farmer's truth: seeds planted on unplowed ground will never produce a harvest. They will lay forever dead, choked out by weeds and lack of depth.

Tear apart the ground, break it up, let everything die away, and then plant? A harvest is coming. A little sun, a little rain, and life will triumph, again.

In **Psalms 85:12** it says, "The Lord will indeed give what is good, and our land will yield its harvest." And it is so true.

I don't know your death. I don't know your plow. I don't know your seeds. But I do know my God.

In my life He tore apart my heart with the plow of infertility. All my roots were ripped to bits. The things I thought I needed to survive were broken and left for dead. And yet, some how, some way, what I thought could only bring death, has filled my heart with life.

And I pray, *oh, how I pray*, that the seeds He planted—grace, empathy, beauty, redemption, hope, joy—will multiply and overflow and feed nations, through my life and yours.

FAITH IN LIFE AND DEATH

WordSnack: 2 Kings 4:8-37

I was sitting on the sofa, tears streaming down my face. My words came out stuttered and halting. "I just feel like now it's final. I'll never have a child."

It sounded harsh, even to my own ears. My husband's hand tightened around mine.

The man seated across the room from me sighed heavily. "Actually," he said, "I've been sensing something from the Lord for awhile about this, but I didn't want to say anything in case I was wrong. Truthfully, it was just fear because I don't want anything to be harder for you. But I'm going to say it. You're going to have a child, soon."

I was too tired to laugh, as Sarah did (Genesis 18:12). And too desperate for hope to refute him, as the Shunammite woman did to Elisha in **2 Kings 4**.

Instead, I sat back and thought, *I guess time will prove if it's really You, Lord.*

I wonder, actually, if the Shunammite woman thought something similar. As I read the story it kept hitting me over and over—the way her faith, though sketchy at first, grew and blossomed under the strangest of circumstances.

She did have a baby, you know. A little boy. One who grew up, apparently healthy, until the day his head starting hurting. After his father took him home from the fields, he lay in his mother's lap until afternoon and then died.

Died.

Right there in his mother's lap.

The child of God's promise. Dead.

But somehow, through the years of barrenness, and despite her initial fear at Elisha's prophecy, the Shunammite woman had become a pillar of faith. She laid the boy down on a bed, got up and went after Elisha. She even told his servant, "All is well," when she got there! But then she held her ground and demanded that Elisha return with her to her dead son.

He goes and the child is restored to life.

Her faith just grows from there. We know because we get a little snippet of narrative about her later on (2 Kings 8:1-6), when her land is restored to her through another set of miraculous incidents.

God often uses strange circumstances to bring about miracles. And He builds up our faith through the most trying of times-restoring hope and life, even in the face of death.

I know, because less than a month after that conversation in the living room, we brought our daughter home.

NO FEAR

~

WordSnack: Isaiah 41:1-10

"I fear God's plan for me is somehow less than what I need." I said the words in honesty but everything in me cringed.

It wasn't pretty. It wasn't holy. Some of it wasn't even good.

But the fear was.

I had just faced years of infertility, had found my way back to God's presence, but was still struggling.

After pain comes fear. Always. When a child is buried, fear stalks the next pregnancy. When a marriage disintegrates, fear slinks through remaining relationships. When cancer appears, fear haunts at every bruise and every abnormal test. When infertility crushes dreams, fear licks at every remaining hope.

Fear is a giant that keeps armies cowering and trained warriors hiding.

If it were just us, we would have reason to slink away to safety, but it's not. This giant stands in mockery of the living God. The One who says, "Do not fear for I am with you" **(Isaiah 41:10).**

The One whose thunder defeats armies (2 Kings 19), whose presence tumbles idols (1 Samuel 5). The One who has this unfailing love that remains through all eternity; and whose redemption conquers the gates of hell.

I pray I will learn to know this God the way David did. That I will choose my stones and face this giant with confidence. That I will truly understand that fear is real and present but my God is greater than any weapon used against me.

The only thing I need in life is to bring God glory. Everything else is a mirage. When I cling to this truth over all else, I find that I am whole and fear has been banished.

GRACE PROMISE

WordSnack: Jeremiah 32:36-41

Last night my daughter called me up to her bedroom. "I need you, Mommy," she whispered from the hallway. Of course I went. Turns out she was nearly hyperventilating with worry.

When my husband came home from work last evening, he was well on his way into a rough case of the flu bug. Our dear little drama-queen had her daddy all but dead and in the grave. "It was just the way he spoke, Mommy," she cried into my shirt, "I think they might have been his last words."

We had a little chat about how the flu doesn't usually kill people and how being tired doesn't mean you're dying. Finally she settled down and I tucked her into bed. Just as I stepped toward the doorway she says, "Will you come get me if he does start to die?"

By now I was a little exasperated. "He's not going to die," I told her.

"But," she narrowed her eyes a bit and said very firmly, "you can't know that. No one knows when we're going to die except God. And we're all gonna go sometime."

Thank you, my eight-year-old philosopher.

But in truth, she has a point. We're all going to go sometimes.

I was thinking about this as I read **Jeremiah 32**. The place where God says in verses 36-41, "I will gather them... I will give them one heart and one way... I will make with them an everlasting covenant... I will rejoice in them... I will plant them in faithfulness... with all my heart and all my soul."

We're all on the path to death. Drenched in sin, unable to save ourselves... but God.

God is faithful to make a way where there is no way. We don't have to fear things in this life, or even death itself.

Yup, we're all going to go sometime, but when that time comes, there is an everlasting covenant that I am clinging to: the covenant of grace. *Thank you, Jesus.*

In counting the gifts
He has given me
I SEE HIM.

FINDING HIM

~

WordSnack: John 21:1-14

In **John 21** we find a story of Jesus showing up again. He already had once, you know. He could have said, "Well, y'all had your chance." But He didn't. He just kept showing up, over and over.

It was after His death and resurrection that He walked right into the disciples lives again. They were back on the fishing boat. Back where they started. Their few short years of traveling with the miracle-worker skidding to a sudden halt.

I've been on fishing boats, up there in Alaska where they fish for salmon off Kachemak Bay. They're smelly and wet and when the waves roll, your stomach lurches into your throat. Yet, there is something achingly soothing about them. You're trusting this mighty boat to hold you afloat, and the salty breeze stirs up something that makes you want to keep breathing and keep going. Splash, yank, pull, holler. Repetitive. Hard. Beautiful. The perfect place to go back to when all of life seems to be crashing out of control.

So that is where they went, these fishermen turned preachers turned lost-wanderers.

But it's not working. They can't catch anything. That uncanny sense of where the fish are and how to cast the nets just right is rusty from a three year fishing break. Instead of satisfying their desire for normalcy, they sit in discouragement.

And Jesus shows up, just like He did when He first called them. "Cast your net on the other side," He says.

They do it. Just like that, they listen.

And when they haul in a record setting load, they sit right down and count them. 153.

And they "knew it was the Lord."

When I take time to count the gifts that God places before me, I find Jesus. Every single time.

BITTERNESS MADE SWEET

WordSnack: Exodus 17:1-7

I don't know how many times I've prayed for healing. Begged. Pleaded. *God, if You see me, take these broken pieces and fix them. Please!* Yet, years of infertility and loss have laced my life.

Something changed, though, when I read the story of the bitter waters at Marah in **Exodus 17**.

The Israelites have been in the desert. They had traveled for three days without water and they finally find a spring.

Can you imagine the way the young boys must have run to the edges of the water? Thrust their faces into it? And then jerked back choking and coughing. Bitter water. Nothing to sate their deep thirst.

They grumbled. Just as I grumble when I taste bitterness. Especially after years in the desert. Three years without babies and I started grumbling because the promise was right there in front of me—but when I grabbed onto it, bitterness embraced me.

In those moments, when all I can taste is bitterness, can I remember who this Lord is whom I serve?

He is Jehovah-Ropheka. The Lord who heals me. The One who takes my bitterness and makes it sweet.

I look at my newly adopted daughter every morning. She stumbles down the stairway in her pink flannel nightgown, black hair snarled around her face. If she sees me doing my devotional reading, she'll come quiet and curl up on the couch beside me.

Years and years of bitterness—far more than the three which I thought would kill me—and finally, Jehovah-Ropheka has placed the wood in the water. Bitter becomes sweet. And I know again today that He is good. And I know that I need Him. I know it in a deeper way than I ever could have known it before.

The Lord takes

BITTERNESS

and makes

IT SWEET.

WHEN GOD SPEAKS

WordSnack: 2 Kings 19

I love Biblical history. Truth be told, I love any history, but Biblical history has an added element. When I study the lives of the king and queens and prophets of old, I find me.

It is always startling.

I'm reading about the prophet Isaiah and King Ahaz of Judah, men who seem to be far and distant from this farmer's wife in Northern New York. I'm studying out the story of kingdoms and world domination and God speaking through prophets and the truth hits me square between the eyes. *Every word that God speaks must be accepted or rejected.*

King Ahaz was told by God, "Don't worry about the kingdoms who are threatening to conquer you—in 65 years they will both be gone. They won't succeed in making you a puppet king and ruling your country" (Isaiah 7). But Ahaz, sounding every bit the wise politically-correct King, rejects the word of God.

Of course it makes no difference with God's plan. The kingdoms fall, just as predicted. But Ahaz, in all his worldly wisdom, has given himself in service to the greater kingdom of Assyria and has become the puppet he was working so hard to avoid being.

The amazing thing about this story is that we get to see the alternate ending. King Ahaz dies and his son Hezekiah takes his place. He inherits a kingdom enslaved to Assyria, but Hezekiah is a king who longs to follow God.

Isaiah speaks the word of the Lord, again, and unlike his father, Hezekiah accepts it. When everything in life shouts for him to do something— he falls at the feet of the Creator and begs for the salvation of his people. And God acts.

In one night the enemy is destroyed and Hezekiah did not have to lift a finger (**2 Kings 19**).

This is still true today. God's plan doesn't change depending on my reaction to His word but my place in His plan can and does change.

I have been King Ahaz, in all his political-correctness. I have said, *I don't want to test the Lord* and I've sounded oh, so proper saying it. God has worked, His will has come about, and I've been left watching from the sidelines.

I've aligned myself with the "Assyrians", depending on earthly power to save me, and I have become enslaved to the very thing that I thought would set me free.

But, *oh, the glory,* I have also been King Hezekiah, in all his brokenness. I have bowed low and watched in awe as God has swept in and re-arranged the unconquerable circumstances.

Only Him.

It is only Christ who saves.

All of life depends on my acceptance or rejection of His words.

HOW TO CHANGE YOUR WORLD

WordSnack: Numbers 16::41-50

People are so hard to work with. There are always disagreements, always hurts, always frustrations.

Every church or group that I've been involved with has produced the same outcome. Joy and pain. Both. They are interlocking. It's impossible to have one without the other.

Pain-filled, difficult people fill our churches and our streets. People that lash out at others. Sometimes their anger is deserved, other times they wound innocent parties.

I was reading in **Numbers 16** and came to the place where the Israelites had risen up against Moses and Aaron. They were led by three men who doubted God's anointing on the two leaders and wished it for themselves. They brought such a stir in the community that even after God caused the earth to swallow up the instigators and their families, and brought fire to consume two hundred and fifty other tribal leaders, they still grumbled against God's chosen.

Moses and Aaron were innocent; yet, they made a surprising choice. God told Moses and Aaron to stay away from the assembly of "grumblers" so he could destroy them. Instead of moving away, Aaron took his offering, which God had accepted, and ran into the midst of the people.

Scripture says, "The plague had already started among the people, but Aaron offered the incense and made atonement for them. He stood between the living and the dead, and the plague stopped (**Numbers 16:47-48** NIV)."

Moses and Aaron were aware of one glaring thing: they were no better than the worst grumbler before them. Moses had murdered and run away. Aaron had crafted an idol for the people to worship! They were in need of God's mercy as much as any of the Israelites in front of them.

This too is true for us. We must be aware of our own faults, our own innumerable sins, our God's great mercy on us. We must also be aware that we can stand between the living and the dead!

When we fall on our faces before the Creator, seeing the hurting souls of the people around us instead of their sharp tongues or hurtful actions, and beg for their lives, we are standing between the living and the dead.

Instead of moving ourselves away from this plague infested world, we need to run into the midst of the lost and offer all we have, that God might show mercy on them— as He has on us.

If we can embrace the same humbleness that kept Moses and Aaron from seeing themselves as greater-than. *If* we can grab onto this others-focused heartbeat that runs through Scripture. *If* we can decide that the greatest thing to do in every circumstance is what brings the most glory to God: we will change the world.

May we learn to
eat and drink

OF HIM

every day.

LIFE BREAD

WordSnack: John 6:35–40

I remember a time when I could only get bread to turn out when I followed the recipe perfectly. Measuring. Careful counting. How hot was the water supposed to be again? I would yell questions to my papa as he sat in the living room reading.

Then over time, it changed. I knew the texture of bread. I knew the amount of yeast per cup of flour. I experimented with all kinds of interesting ingredients. Lentils. Kidney beans. Sprouts. White whole wheat. Fresh ground wheat. Spelt. Soaked grains. This and that made its way into my bread. I never followed a recipe because I didn't need one.

I could tell by the smell, by the feel of it, if it was going to turn out. Sometimes I would be kneading and realize, *It's not going to rise.* And my plans would change. Pizza for dinner.

I want to know Jesus and His kingdom the way that I know bread. When I touch life, I want to know what's missing, what's needed—what the point is. Most of all, I want to be the good yeast. The part that makes things rise and grow and be more of what God created them to be.

Jesus spoke many times about "watching" for the yeast of the Pharisees. Just a little bit affects a lot. Words and actions that are contrary to God's truth can spread quickly and work their way into and around—making a sorry mess out of things that are meant to be beautiful.

When I knead bread—turning, working, pounding—I pray. I ask God to put His kingdom inside me, so when I effect things around me (for I will) my gift is more of His Kingdom, more of His truth.

Jesus told us many times that He is the bread of life. The sustaining food for our existence. "Then Jesus declared, 'I am the bread of life. Whoever comes to me will never go hungry, and whoever believes in me will never be thirsty'" (**John 6:35**).

May we all learn to eat and drink of Him, every day.

MORE THAN YOU CAN BEAR

WordSnack: Deuteronomy 20:1-4

She said the words with an ashen face, her hands clenched in defeat. "I know God doesn't give us more than we can bear, but *I can't bear this.*"

And I heard her. Every word. Every clenched fist. Every tear.

Life offers pieces of broken pain that far outweigh our ability to endure. This often believed idea that "God doesn't give us more than we can bear", comes, I think, from a verse that says, "And God is faithful; he will not let you be tempted beyond what you can bear" (1 Corinthians 10:13).

Being tempted and enduring pain are two very different things. In temptation, God always gives us a way out. In pain, God often calls us to walk right through.

I have heard so many stories. The ones that tell of buried babies, broken dreams, ravaging cancer, and countless horrible steps through debilitating pain. The tales are filled with life-altering experiences that have left so many weak and lost in the wake.

I don't want you to think that God hasn't kept His end of the bargain. I want you to understand: *you will face more than you can bear.* It will happen.

Life is full of rough edges and harsh realities. You were never meant to battle them alone, and you don't have to be strong enough.

Following God is not a formula to free yourself from pain and difficulty. It never has been. Following God is about giving glory and honor to the only One who deserves it; even when you have to give that glory through broken whispers.

You will face more than you can bear. When you're standing in battle, depleted of your own strength, He will be the arm that keeps your sword held up. He will be the voice that whispers truth into lies. He will be the strength at your back, the defeater of the enemy, the glorious Redeemer.

In **Deuteronomy 20**, the Israelites are reminded that when they go to war, they are not alone. "For the LORD your God is the one who goes with you to fight for you against your enemies to give you victory" (**Deuteronomy 20:4** NIV). They are reminded that the great I AM is the one who will win every battle.

We can't win alone. Isn't that the truth that we so often forget? We flail about struggling and thinking, *I should be strong enough. I should be godly enough. I should be able to find victory. I should be able to face life without crumbling.* No, friends, we shouldn't… because if we could, we wouldn't need a Savior.

BE TRANSFORMED

WordSnack: Romans 12:1-2

I truly believe that God is all-powerful, all-knowing and omnipresent, but sometimes I don't act like it. Instead, I act like I have to accomplish things in my own power because God can't or won't.

I act like God has forgotten or doesn't care.

I act like God isn't present.

Oh, Lord, forgive me.

I want my life to be an accurate picture of my beliefs. What good is it to believe the truth if you don't live it?

My hope and goal is to align my beliefs with my actions. Not just outward actions but inwardly; my thoughts, feelings, hopes and fears.

And I don't just mean when it comes to the big things—I want the little things to match up as well. I don't want to just read the Scripture and think, "Yes, yes. I believe that." I do believe! Yet, I want more. When it says, "Do not conform any longer to the pattern of this world, but be transformed by the renewing of your mind" (**Romans 12:2**), I want to read it, believe and be transformed. Repeatedly. Daily. Over and over.

How easy it is to just accept Scripture because that's what we've been taught, but never allow it to go deeper. It never cuts in. It never radically changes.

We are called to present our bodies as "living sacrifices" as a spiritual act of worship. In my heart, I need to be bowing low, surrendering to Him, again and again.

It doesn't matter if I've been a Christian for five minutes, five years, or half a century. Every time I read the words of God, I want to be changed a little more into His image.

WHEN LIFE GETS HARD

WordSnack: 2 Corinthians 12:1-10

Sometimes life clouds right up with hard.

I'm tired and there are kids whining and pulling at my skirt, but none of them were born from my body. Instead of being the mother I desire to be, I find myself caring for other women's babies. There is paperwork that needs to be filled out, my husband is hungry and in a hurry, the bills are stacking up, my hair is frizzed out, my sister is moving too many miles away from me, there are bills to juggle and… I forget.

There is a God who longs to walk through every single moment with me. He cares about all the small details. When I drop my head and lift my hands, saying again, "Lord, give me grace." He answers. He is not alien to the feeling of being overwhelmed. He is not disappointed in my weakness—on the contrary! "But He said to me, 'My grace is sufficient for you, for my power is made perfect in weakness'" (**2 Corinthians 12:9**).

God delights in meeting us right where we are. He rejoices in showing His strength, in pulling us from the depths.

His whispers of hope and faith and truth start filling the kitchen. When I voice my need for Him, my ears are opened to His presence.

Hours later I am sitting while the four little babies who came to visit me are all snuggled in, softly snoring. There is music playing quietly. There are apples and cucumbers and a juicy cantaloupe covering my counters. Chai tea is heating on the stove, filling the air with the scent of cinnamon and ginger. Grace and grace and more grace.

I wish I could plaster a sign to my forehead that says, "Have you asked God for grace today?" I need Him. Today. Tomorrow. The next day. New every morning.

"Therefore I will boast all the more gladly about my weaknesses, so that Christ's power may rest on me" (**2 Corinthians 12:9**).

RE-BUILDER OF BROKEN LIVES

WordSnack: Nehemiah 1:4-11

Nehemiah was a working man. Cupbearer to the King of Persia, he served the highest official in the land.

When God burdened Nehemiah's heart with the condition of his homeland Israel, he wasn't looking around for the most capable man. Nehemiah was a cupbearer, not a builder. Yet, God saw something in Nehemiah.

As you read through the book of Nehemiah you find him facing giants of many kinds. Opposition from all sides. Still he continues through it all. Persevering. He didn't find the strength within himself but in his God.

He rebuilds the walls and in so doing, rebuilds the lives of the remnant of Israel, the last of God's chosen people.

This isn't a new story. God does this over and over.

He saw a king within the shepherd boy, David. A brave queen behind the pretty face of Esther. A leader and warrior in the youngest of the smallest tribe in Gideon. The foundation of the New Testament church inside the unstableness of Peter. The builder of that church in the destroyer Saul, who became Paul.

What does this say to us? We're usable to God. Even with all our brokenness. All our sins and failures and fears.

Not because we have the ability within ourselves. But rather, because He chooses to *use* us, as weak and feeble as we are.

All it takes is an open heart. One that weeps at the destruction of the church. One that recognizes our failures and our desperate need for Jesus Christ. One that is willing to say, "I have to try and if I perish, I perish."

May we all learn to walk this road. May we learn to be the "Nehemiahs" of this day and age. The re-builders of broken walls and broken lives, for the glory of Him who redeems our weaknesses by showing His strength.

WE SERVE A GOD

who redeems our weakness
by showing His strength.

WHEN BLIND EYES SEE

WordSnack: John 9:1-41

Most of the healings that are recorded in the gospels start with someone asking to be healed. Except this one. This story starts with a question about sin. "Rabbi, who sinned…?" (**John 9:2**) Whose sin caused this man to be born blind? Is it his fault? His parents' fault?

What must the man have been thinking? I know what I would have been thinking. *I have enough sin to be forced into a thousand lifetimes of blindness. Even that wouldn't begin to pay the debt I owe. I don't know who these people are that are asking but I know this: I am a sinner.*

This Rabbi begins to speak of something different. Not the ugliness of sin but the beauty of God working. Not un-payable debts owed but the gift of light shining in darkness.

Then spit and dust. Reminds me of the beginning, at Eden, as the dust of the earth was formed into a man and the breath of God brought life. Just like then, life comes. This time in the form of sight.

The once-blind-but-now-seeing man stands before the Pharisees and testifies to truth. In the face of the men who had always been above him, who had judged him and his parents for his blindness, who had written him off as a worthless beggar, he stood fast. "One thing I do know, that though I was blind, now I see" (**John 9:25**).

In the face of the answers that shame them, they scorn him. He is labeled a sinner, again. Thrown out. Pushed back to being the worthless beggar unworthy of being near the righteous.

Jesus comes back and asks the question. "Do you believe?" It's the question every person in the world has to answer, and this man answers right. "'Lord, I believe,' and he worshiped him" (**John 9:38**).

The worthless beggar becomes a son of God. The sinner is washed clean and made righteous. The lost are found and the blind can see.

Jesus says, "I have come into this world, so that the blind will see and those who see will become blind" (**John 9:39**).

This is the God I serve. My God. The one who makes blind eyes see.

My eyes. The ones that get trapped in darkness and hidden in sin and covered in pain. The eyes that try so desperately to see for themselves. The ones that, to my horror and shame, have so often been standing in the place of the Pharisees.

He makes them see.

Those who claim to see without Jesus will remain lost in blindness, guilty. Those who acknowledge their blindness and admit their need for Him will be healed.

Oh, glory.

In Him we know

THE DAWN.

NEW LiFE

WordSnack: Psalm 34:22

With evening comes new life on the farm. One of the two cows left to freshen drops a heifer calf. She's born with stubborn built in and fights the rope I slip around her neck. Her muscles tense and I laugh at her antics. Her mama calms her down with swift licks of her tongue.

Life is born in blood.

I scrape the after-birth into the gutter, pleased that she cleaned so easily. The baby calf looks at me through large brown eyes.

It is evening, late, yet I feel like I just took the first breath of morning. In **Psalms 34:22** we are told, "The Lord redeems the life of His servants." The promise settles into my bones.

Sometimes life is dirty and messy, sometimes even bloody, but, in Him, there is new life, light, morning—even when everything seems pitch black.

Night may be stretching across our world, but in Him we know of the dawn. There is no fear, for we serve a God who does the miraculous, who defies the world's order.

In defeat, He brings victory, with dry bones He builds mighty armies, and in death, *oh, in death,* we actually find life.

That's the wonder of knowing the Savior.

That is the ultimate redemption.

THE SINS OF SODOM

WordSnack: Ezekiel 16:48-50

The speaker says, "Let's turn to Ezekiel 16."

I smiled. I love that chapter. The imagery of the baby, left to die in a field, and the Savior who comes along and proclaims, "Live! Live!" But that's not the part he reads. As we're turning, pages ruffling through the sanctuary, he asks, "Tell me, what was it that caused Sodom to be destroyed by fire?"

No one speaks but we're all thinking, *it was her sexual immorality.* Of course. It says so... doesn't it?

"Now this was the sin of your sister Sodom: She and her daughters were arrogant, overfed and unconcerned; they did not help the poor and needy" (**Ezekiel 16:49**).

The roaring starts. Did he not just read about... me?

Arrogance? My pride has stopped me in my tracks. Overfed? My gluttony for food, clothing, *things* is horrifying. Unconcerned? My ability to shut my eyes to the lost souls around me is troubling. Poor and needy? When was the last time I sacrificed, really sacrificed, something I valued to help those in need?

What is the difference between me and Sodom? Aren't we the same? Mirror images? Except. *Oh, yes.* I have learned to kneel, to bow low. And this is the thing that sets me apart.

Unless we humble ourselves, we're just as guilty as the next. Unless we cling to the cross, we're lost.

Today, again, the scales of blindness fall. My eyes are soothed with salve and my hands grasp the gold that is refined, the thing that makes me truly rich. I am no different unless I kneel. And when I bow low, I am clothed and fed and I receive my sight.

My pride is slaughtered. I joyfully share what I have with those around me. My heart is turned to the lost and my eyes are opened to the needs I can meet in my community, in my home, and in the world.

Lord, keep my eyes clear and my heart set on you.

WHEN LIFE FEEDS YOU LIES

WordSnack: Psalm 119:81-88

Hard days still come, sweeping in and leaving me lost and trembling. The voice says, *"It's only because... If only you had _____ then you would have what you desire."*

The words that fill the blank vary on the day but they all spell the same thing: *failure.*

I'm learning not to debate the lies anymore. It only leaves my ear tuned to the negative, only leaves my emotional state teetering on depression.

There is only one thing to do in the face of failure: cling to what is living and breathing and lasting.

My hurts are only bearable when they are buried in the Word.

In those moments, the only thing I know to do is open to **Psalm 119.** The longest chapter in the Bible. Did you know that almost every single verse references the Word of God?

- Your Word.
- Your law.
- Your statutes.
- Your promise.
- Your commands.
- His way.
- His precepts.
- His decrees.

It's like one long song that points out the wonder of the voice of God. In the reading, in the words flowing through the quiet house, the lies are silenced.

He is. And His Word still shines light into dark places.

OH, FAITHLESS HEART

WordSnack: Jeremiah 3:22

I'm not sure why that day was so hard, but it was. A day when the thoughts of all-that-could-be got lost in the reality of all-that-wasn't. My husband kept asking what was wrong and I kept opening my mouth but not finding the words.

Is it possible to explain that the "wrong" is only a complete and total lack of faith?

I wandered around the barn doing chores, with my mind trapped in faithlessness. I knelt to put a milking unit on Rosie and tears dripped onto the golden straw at my feet. *I hate this part of me*, I thought. *I hate weakness and feeling lost and panic attacks.* Why can't I just trust that God really will take care of me?

Oh, Lord. Here I am, still trying to take your place. I'd rather lose my deepest dreams by choice than trust you with the ability to answer my prayers with a "no."

Oh, faithless heart!

Can't I remember truth? The knowledge burns. I can have a hundred altars in my past and not truly know God in the present, if I am not surrendering to Him today.

When my face bows low, He comes. Faithful every moment. He whispers comfort that seeks me out and pulls back my blinders with love. "Return, O faithless sons; I will heal your faithlessness" (**Jeremiah 3:22**).

Oh, what a promise! Oh, joy! Oh, hope! Oh, redemption!
He heals. Even my faithlessness.

My tongue tastes glory. My soul trembles. And once again, I find wholeness.

When I surrender

HE COMES.

FINDING WORSHIP

WordSnack: John 4:21-24

Walmart was crowded. People swirling through, grabbing fresh loaves of bread and Florida oranges and stocking stuffers. My own bag of last minute essentials was tucked beside my purse in the cart.

It's a tradition, started years ago now. The group of us stumbled upon each other in the mini dining area at Walmart and because it was Christmas, and we often joke about living in a musical, someone started a carol. People stopped and stared of course, but that never slowed us down. In fact, it egged a few people on. If someone is watching, then how about a show?

Carols and four-part harmony and a few twirls.

The workers begged us to come back again the next year. So we did. And the year after and the year after.

I didn't make it every year but I did that Christmas Eve. I stood, beside the display of dinner rolls and joined in, laughing through a slightly misguided attempt at "Carol of the Bells." Then we switched to "O Come, All Ye Faithful" and it happened.

I might not have noticed except for that just a few nights before we had been talking about it. Meg, with her smile dancing and that glow in her eye, saying that she had found worship again. "It's been so long," she said. She spun her fork through the melting ice cream on her plate and I felt her words down to my bones.

Worship had become something I did because I choose to live a lifestyle of worship, which is good. But somewhere along the way, I lost the freedom. I lost the sense of entering in. When she spoke, my heart starting beating wildly. Perhaps it was out there, somewhere, the freedom and depth I longed to find again.

When Jesus spoke to the Samaritan woman in **John 4,** He voiced the promise of it. "Yet a time is coming and has now come when the true worshipers will worship the Father in the Spirit and in truth, for they are the kind of worshipers the Father seeks."

In Spirit and in truth, He tells us. In our hearts, somewhere deep inside, worshiping and *believing.* But, I'll be honest, sometimes I falter. I forget. My heart disconnects with my understanding.

Yet, I found it again on the second chorus of "O Come, All Ye Faithful" in the middle of Walmart on that Christmas Eve. In the moment between, *oh, come let us adore Him*, and *we'll give Him all the glory*, something broke free.

I don't know if other people felt it but I did. And I stood on holy ground, right there beside the three shelves of dinner rolls.

I want to live worship. Yes, I want to live a lifestyle of worship. But I want to be filled with moments too. Moments that I can carve in the words and mark deep into my heart: *I was here and He was here.*

For He alone is worthy.

MORNING COMES

WordSnack: Psalm 130

Some days run hard together and the sun seems to disappear even while it shines bright. It was one of these days when my husband showed up, took my hand, and said, "Let's go on a mini-vacation."

We spent the night at a hotel, one that sat right on the water where we could watch the last shades of pink slide out of sight into the ripples spread by the wind. After the light was gone, I took a long hot bath and prayed that muffled tears wouldn't wake my husband.

They were happy tears. Sort of.

The kind that comes and you're fine, just sad, but okay and happy? Of course. You're blessed and provided for and loved… and hurting. All at once and together and the same.

He was awake when I slipped into bed. "Read to me," he said, so I clicked on the light and reached for my Bible and read the words I had underlined so many times. "Oh, Israel, put your hope in the Lord, for with the Lord is unfailing love and with him is full redemption."

"Where is that found?" he asks.

"**Psalm 130**," I say, turning the page for him to see.

"Read the whole chapter to me." He settles back against the pillow.

So I read and the words drift off me and float away. He sleeps at the sound of my voice and I quietly close the book and click out the light.

The clock reads 5:00 when I open my eyes again. My husband is snoring and sleep has evaporated so I slide from the covers and slip into a skirt. It is this bright silly thing that made me smile when I bought it, the way the stripes of color seem to swirl when I walk.

A jacket over my shoulders and I step outside to wander. Frost painted the ground, thicker as I neared the water's edge. I stepped onto the dock and almost slipped, the icy whiteness stealing traction. Two steps, three steps, a cloud breaks and the sun makes me blink. I stand there, quiet, watching the frost melt away.

A verse comes to mind, the one that I paused at the night before, wondering why such a strange line was repeated. "My soul waits for the Lord, more than watchmen wait for the morning, more than watchmen wait for the morning" (**Psalm 130:6**).

The last bit of frost is melting, the sun is so warm it is burning a pattern on my face. It comes, you know. The morning comes. And the watchmen, they know that morning will arrive. Light will break through and darkness will flee and morning always comes.

No matter how strong the powers of darkness seem, the Kingdom of God is advancing.

We wait with assurance. With knowledge. With the power of knowing the darkness will leave. Like watchmen wait for the morning, we wait.

I hear the click of a camera shutter and spin around to see my husband standing on the balcony with my camera in his hands. "You look like your Mama," he says, voice echoing across the silent water. I wrap my arms around myself and call for him to come. So he leaves the warmth of the room and visits the coolness of morning.

We walk on the boardwalk and talk about mornings and Christ's return and hope that is unchanging, that never dies, that burns deep and grows us upward.

Walking through the darkness of winter can feel like death at times, but the dormant season is needed to produce a harvest. Eventually morning light will touch the fertile ground and life will spring forth.

So we journey on, waiting expectantly, because it always comes. The morning always comes.

THROUGH WEAKNESS

WordSnack: Judges 6:11-18

Sometimes I cringe at my own weakness. I can't get things right, no matter how hard I try. I am continually overwhelmed and lost, floundering through life.

Yet, today, when I was reading the story of Gideon, God caught hold of my heart again. Right there in **Judges 6:15,** God calls Gideon and he answers. "But Lord," Gideon replied, "how can I rescue Israel? My clan is the weakest in the whole tribe of Manasseh and I am the least in my entire family."

And we know the rest of the story. How God used the least of all, from the weakest tribe, to lead 300 men against thousands—and win.

We serve a God who chooses the least. The weakest.

So perhaps He will use me—with all my scars, my still-healing-wounds, my pains, my stumbling blocks, my desperate thirst… my agonizing need for Him.

And somehow, perhaps, I will be used to rescue a part of God's Israel. Maybe, somewhere out there in the vastness of this world there is a person who is scarred, wounded, in pain, stumbling around, and dying of thirst. Someone who, not despite my weakness, but *through it*, will be able to hear my words about Him. And another child of the King will be carried into the kingdom where they can finally quench their thirst by the side of the fountain of living water.

And you, with any weakness you carry, He longs to use you as well. For anything given to Him can be utilized for His glory, even the things on which we place no value.

God will use me,
not despite my weakness
BUT THROUGH IT.

WHEN FAITH FALTERS

WordSnack: Luke 22:39-46

Sometimes life feels like a sucker-punch to the gut. The moment when air rushes out and doesn't come back fast enough, when I'm unable to speak, to think, to move.

Recently I felt this, and leaned in close to the Body. I whispered the story, quiet and pain-filled.

It was my friend Delite who answered, our lifetime friendship laying the foundation for her to speak with gentle firmness, "Remember the testing of our faith develops perseverance, which in turn is making you mature and complete, not lacking anything!"

In hushed agony, I responded, "But what if I don't have any faith to test?"

I was too afraid to pray. Too scared to believe. Too broken to even dream. Faith was but a distant hope, as untouchable as the stars.

"Don't be ridiculous," my sister-in-law, Brianna, chimes in, "faith is just choosing to believe. You do it all the time."

I feel the shudders start, breath seeping in, oxygen inflating my lungs once more.

Her voice continues, "The thing is, the Lord loves to act. He does. But first, you have to ask. And sometimes the asking is hard work. It's praying in the garden and sweating blood."

I like the thought of things being easy, don't you? I don't want to be the one in the garden, sweating blood. I want to be the one watching the miracles.

And when the miracles don't come right away? I want to give up and move on. I want to read a novel and let my mind escape. I want to pretend like I never asked for a miracle, never really hoped for one at all. I want to do anything except bruise my knees and cry out my agony, because it hurts. *Oh, how it hurts.* And I might not like the answers and I sure enough don't like this garden.

This garden that looks like loneliness, where it seems like all your friends are sleeping. This garden that looks like tears. This garden that looks like fasting and praying, denying self, pushing forward, exhaustion. This garden that looks like hard work, that looks like loss and wondering and heart wrenching cries of, *"My God, my God, why hast Thou forsaken me?"*

This garden of death that leads to… life?

Oh, friends, if there is going to be life from death, there has to be a garden. If our lives are truly going to reflect Christ, then there will be moments of betrayal and hurt and loss. There will be moments when we just can't breathe. There will be moments of death.

But those moments are only paving the way for life.

So let us persevere, right through this garden time. Let perseverance finish its work in us that we might become mature and complete—not lacking anything. And isn't that a promise to cling to?

He has
GOOD
in store for me.

LISTEN AND FOLLOW

WordSnack: Proverbs 3:5-6

Yesterday afternoon my husband drove the skidsteer to get a round bale for the cattle. They're all out to pasture now, but we're still supplementing their grazing with hay. When he got near the gate, he jumped down and talked to our daughter. "I need you to open and shut the gate for me," he told her. Step by step, he showed her how to lift the latch, pull it open and then shut it tight.

"But Daddy," she said, "I'm too scared! What if the cows get me?"

He looked her right in the eye, "If you listen to me and follow my directions exactly, I will always be between you and the cattle. You will never be in danger."

I was reminded of that story this morning as I read **Proverbs 3**. Solomon is talking to his son, telling him to listen and follow his directions. Then he gives some of the most important advice any of us will ever receive. "Trust in the Lord with all your heart, and do not rely on your own understanding. In all your ways acknowledge him, and he will make your paths smooth."

The word "acknowledge" here is actually the Hebrew word *yada* which means to know and be known by.

We are called to know and be known by God in everything we do. When we listen and follow (know Him), He will lead and guide us through every step of our journey (where we are known by Him)!

And just as my daughter was perfectly safe when she was following her daddy's directions, even though she didn't fully understand all that was happening around her, so is my heart perfectly safe when I am following my Father's directions.

Trust Yahweh, the verse says. Trust the One-True-God. Trust Abba-Father. Trust the One who has good in store for me.

I MUST DECREASE

~

WordSnack: John 3:22-30

The day was hot and sticky, like a film was in the air that rested on everything. It was the first time I had seen her in almost a year. She called me over, right outside the grocery store, and told me all about the past months. About the new baby that filled her life and arms, about the way her relationships were growing better, the way God was working in her.

And honestly, I felt a bit perturbed.

See, I was the one who gave up time for her and cared for her son when she could not. I was the one who sacrificed and said the hard things and stared her right in the face and told her that God had a plan for her that didn't involve getting beat up by a drunk boyfriend.

Then one day she disappeared from my life. I didn't know what happened or where she was. For a year, my story didn't intersect with hers.

When it did, on that humid summer day, I wanted to roll my eyes at God. "Why," I wanted to say, "did I have to wade through the rough stuff without getting a chance to be part of the turn-around? Why did I get the crap and other friends get the joy?"

I gave her a hug goodbye and then climbed into the car, with the questions swirling through my head. It was there, with sweat dripping down my back, that I felt the answer; the truth I needed to face.

John the Baptist faced it centuries ago. His disciples came to him and basically said, "Hey, John, remember that guy, Jesus, whom you testified about? Well, He's baptizing people over on the other side of the Jordan, and all your followers are going to Him."

And John looked at them and said, "He must become greater and greater, and I must become less and less" (**John 3:30** NLT).

All the people that I minister to and encourage and disciple? The hope is that they will walk away from me and go find Jesus. He must increase and I must decrease.

Because I can't save anyone. I couldn't save her.

Only Jesus can.

It doesn't matter how much of the picture I get to show up in. It doesn't matter if I ever see the good stuff. All that matters is that I remain faithful to speak His name and prepare the way for His truth to enter hearts.

Sometimes that means all I get is the dirty part. All I see are the filthy feet that need washing. Jesus says, "If you follow me, you will do as I do." I'll bend low and wash the feet of those around me.

In doing so, glory will rest on Him. Not me. And that's okay, because it's not about me.

God's grace poured over me that afternoon as I drove home. I felt His gentle, loving presence. I knew the whole truth: as He becomes greater, I am blessed more than I could ever be otherwise. He is Alpha and Omega, the beginning and the end. With His presence comes all that is good.

We need to learn to let go, to be willing to do the dirty work and never be named as the one who cleaned up. To wash the dishes and care for the children; do the hard stuff, and then be ignored. The whole point of it is not to bring glory to ourselves, but to show the world who Jesus is. We need to take John the Baptist's words and make them our own.

"Jesus must become greater and greater, and I must become less and less."

FACING STORMS

~

WordSnack: Matthew 14:24-33

I knew the God who commands the wind and waves was more than capable of calming the seas in my life. He could heal my pain, ease my trials, touch my broken body, but for some reason, He seemed to be sleeping.

Did I need to pray more? Believe more? Why was God allowing this when I had surrendered all to follow Him? What more did He want?

I read the story of the storm in Matthew 8. The disciples, fearing for their lives, woke up the sleeping Jesus. "Oh, you of little faith," He said to them, "why are you afraid?"

That's me, Lord, that's me. I'm terrified. Won't you wake up and calm this storm?

Eventually He did, but not until I walked many years through stormy seas. It wasn't until I reread the book of Matthew again that I began to understand why. There in **Matthew 14** there is another storm beating the disciples' boat, causing them trouble and fear. This time Jesus comes to them, walking on the water, and when they cry out in terror He says, "Don't fear. I AM." Because He is and He always will be.

This is after Jesus fed the 5,000, after five loaves and two fish became more than enough. Even then the disciples hadn't understood. They had treated Christ's miraculous gift as commonplace. Their hearts were calloused from the abundance of miracles taking place around them.

So Jesus went away to pray, and the disciples left in their boat, and another storm stirred up from the depths of the Sea of Galilee.

Once again, the disciples were the ones in need. It was their lives on the line. It was their humanity that stared them in the face… and Jesus came.

Just like He does for all of us.

He walked through the storm to bring calmness and peace. The kind that goes beyond understanding.

And there, in the 33rd verse, I find my answer. "And those in the boat knelt and worshiped Him, saying, Truly You are the Son of God!"

I knew who Jesus was long before storms buffeted my life. I knew about His love and His grace and His precious blood that spilled to save me. I worshiped Him for what I was told He was. Yet, somehow, in the midst, my heart grew calloused. *Jesus is the Son of God.* Yup. He is.

Then the storms raged. I was battered and shaken and fearful, and Jesus walked right into the middle of it all and spoke peace. It was then that I knelt hard and fast, raised shaking hands, and lifted my voice to say, "Truly, truly, you are the Son of God!"

I tasted a storm, and it was *my* life on the line, *my* heart that was broken, *my* eyes that were blind. It was *my* life that was spared, *my* heart that was healed, *my* eyes that were opened.

Now I don't worship Him because I believe He is who someone said He is; I worship Christ because I *know* He is who He says He is.

Like the disciples, I needed to taste my own humanity, my own inability to save myself, so I could really understand what it was that God was offering. Life, peace, hope.

"Fear not," He said to me, "I AM."

All His words are true. Whether you're experiencing a hurricane or a short squall, any life-storm is difficult to swallow. If you're like me, all you want is comfort, but true comfort is only found in knowing Christ.

So lift up your head, look at the cross. He's not just the God who created the earth, He's the God who created your heart. He is worthy of all your worship. Through the darkness of your storm, watch for His presence, listen for His voice. He'll be telling you the same thing. "Do not fear. I AM."

So bow low and give Him glory, for He is.

WHAT ABOUT HER?

WordSnack: John 21:18-22

Some days are easier than others. Some days I wake up and life is filled with sunshine and my husband is wonderful and my heart is content.

And then comes the day when the teenager is pregnant, the baby is being raised by a grandmother, and the mother who doesn't want to be bothered aborts.

Those are the days when I pound my fists into my pillow. When I cry out the unending question into the dark red walls of my bedroom, "Why, God? Why does she get babies? Why?"

It's agony. This screaming monster inside that claws to control my thoughts, my voice, my actions.

"Why does the one who misuses your gift, get it? Why does the one who would treasure it, not? What part of that makes sense in your all-knowing mind?" I can't resist pointing. I can't resist speaking into the shadow that seems to be consuming my heart. "What about her, God?"

And the phrase brings to mind another person who spoke similar words. His name was Peter. Rock. He was often short-tempered and rash. He probably spoke rapid-fire questions and wondered what was wrong with God's all-knowing mind. Especially when Jesus told him about the death that would come to him. A death where Peter would stretch out his hands and be led where he did not want to go. And afterward, Peter saw another disciple—the one that Jesus loved— and he said, "Wait, what about him?"

And Jesus said, "What's that to you? You must follow me" (**John 21:22**).

My heart slows. My questions stop. Jesus answered Peter that day, but he also answered me.

"Why does she get babies?" I asked.

"What's that to you? You must follow me," He answered.

I must get up, take up my cross, and serve Him. I must give

glory and honor to God. What is it to me, who receives the gift of children? It is not my call, not my right, not my business.

Peter was the rock God built His church upon. Peter, who died a criminal's death, though innocent. Whose wife was martyred as well. Peter, who had to give up and give up and give up. When he pointed and questioned, Jesus answered him straight. *What's that to you? You follow Me.*

And I'm the girl who loves God and wants to serve Him. And so far? I cannot bear a child. I've been asked to give up and give up and give up. And when I point and question, Jesus answers me straight. *What's that to you? You follow Me.*

The answer echoes around me. It closes in and leaves me quiet and humble. It turns out that I'm not God and I don't get to pick. Low and behold, it's not even my business.

My business is simple: to follow Him.

And your question, friend? Jesus answers yours as well.

Why does she get a husband who actually works at their marriage? Why does she have a husband who is faithful? Why does she get a husband at all?

Why does she get a job that she loves? Why does she get to stay home? Why does she have extra spending money?

Why does she have extended family that helps her? Why does she have a mother who cares?

Why does she have good health? Why... Why...

"What's that to you?" He says, "You follow Me."

WHAT ARE YOU AFRAID OF?

WordSnack: 2 Thessalonians 3:1-5

A few nights ago I sat with my new daughter and she whispered fears into the dark of her bedroom. They were hushed and sorrow-filled, created by real events and knowledge.

Just like the fears I battle, the ones I've learned from life-experiences that left me hurting and empty. The ones that are reasonable and realistic. The ones I can leave to churn and thrash around until they burn into anger—fiery and hot and capable of defending my home and my life, but not my heart.

I look down at my daughter, with the moonlight tracing patterns on her face, and I don't want that for her. Anger only burns the person holding it. Fear only cripples the person clinging to it.

So we start singing, because what else is there to do but sing?

Psalm 46:1-2 is sung as we tuck the blankets in. Hebrews 13:6 is whispered as I brush the hair back from her face. At breakfast the next morning, as the eggs are frying in the pan and toast is browning, II Timothy 4:18 dances through the kitchen.

On the dark evenings, when fears come and we can't seem to stop them, Psalm 56:3 fills the room with comfort.

When fearful words come racing through, in the middle of lessons and heart-shaping moments of teaching, Isaiah 41:10 becomes the theme song.

Through the darkest moments we sing John 16:33, because "in this world we will have trouble but take heart! He has overcome the world." He brings peace, which deprives the world of its power to harm us. He whispers John 14:27 into the recesses of our hearts.

Last Sunday, when the morning didn't go as planned and we didn't know if we'd make it to church or be stuck on the side of the road, she looked over at me and started singing **2 Thessalonians 3:3**. We smiled because it's true. God is faithful. And we're protected. All the things we think matter so much, they really don't at all.

When we make it to church and they announce the children's

trivia question, she bounces out of her seat and waves her hand wildly. **2 Thessalonians 3:3**. The one we've been singing all morning long. "I knew the answer," she tells me. "It was easy as puddin' pie. He'll protect me from the evil one."

I laugh because she's turning into my daughter, sure as shootin', and we're figuring out this fear thing—both of us together.

God did not give us a spirit of fear, but of power and love and of sound mind. He created us to live as Sarah's daughters, doing what it right and not giving way to fear. He created us to live, not be crippled and burnt by fear and anger.

"Peace, I leave with you" (John 14:27).

That's what He said. I believe Him.

And to you, the one who is struggling with fears chasing, His peace is for you as well.

NO REASON TO FEAR

WordSnack: Proverbs 1:33

There we were, sitting around her kitchen table. Her whole house is warmth and comfort and gentleness. She asks the questions everyone should ask. She looks right at me and digs right into the deepest-truest part. "And how are you doing, really? Are you struggling with fear?"

Many people have mentioned it, but in statements. "I'm sure you're nervous, but it'll all be okay." They say the words and let me accept them as my own.

She doesn't. She asks the question and lets it dangle there in the air between us, waiting.

Am I struggling with fear? *Yes.* Yes, of course.

It's good for me to admit it. It's good for me to stumble through a few random lists.

It's good when, afterward, she stands up and grabs her iPad, "There's a verse…" she says. Then we read it together and truth sinks down deep into my bones.

I went searching for it the next morning, as the sunlight streaked through the bright kitchen window. **Proverbs 1:33**. I read it, again and again. "…but whoever listens to me will dwell secure, and will be at ease, without dread of disaster."

She explained it so well that evening. How it doesn't say that disaster won't come. How it doesn't promise protection from everything bad.

No, it promises security; knowing the end, despite the middle junk. It promises ease and peace, not having to be afraid of the "what-ifs" and "might-coulds."

I sit and I eat my fill of this promise: when I am listening to Christ, I can be at ease, without dread of tomorrow.

When I am listening to Christ
I have no reason to fear

TOMORROW.

NO CONDEMNATION

WordSnack: Romans 8:1-2

I was at college, talking to my professor about my end of the semester project: an in-depth study of one chapter of the Bible. I was so excited about it. The chapter I chose was Isaiah 58, where God talks about true fasting.

"My roommates and I are doing a fast right now," I said in my flurried speech, "so I am really excited about digging into this topic."

My professor, who was listening intently, suddenly frowned. I noticed the change of expression, assumed I was taking up too much of his time, and excused myself.

The next day in class, he took quite some time talking about the passage in Matthew 6, where Jesus is teaching about fasting in secret. He looked pointedly at me and said, "I feel that anyone who announces they are fasting has then nullified the fast."

I was horrified.

I felt condemnation to the tips of my toes.

Although I had been so excited about the project, I know the paper I turned in was less than mediocre, despite my ability to write. It was laced with embarrassment and dry as dirt.

Afterwards, I couldn't remember that situation without my face flushing; until the year I decided to start memorizing **Romans 8**. "Therefore, there is now no condemnation for those who are in Christ Jesus, because through Christ Jesus the law of the Spirit of life set me free from the law of sin and death."

One day I was in the middle of reciting the passage when I felt God still my heart. I remembered the situation and I felt God clearly say, *You've been carrying this weight of condemnation for years—feeling embarrassment for publicly sharing about your fast, but you've never asked me what I think about it.*

His words shocked me, but they were so true! I hadn't asked Him. Instead, I just accepted the weight of condemnation someone offered me right onto my shoulders and carried it away, for years. After all, they were using Scripture to pour the weight onto me, therefore, they must be right… right?

But, of course, when I asked God the question, His answer was very different. It was **Romans 8:1.** "There is now no condemnation."

Turns out, God sees far more than man can see. He sees and judges our hearts. Where there is sin, we're responsible to repent and be cleansed. Where there is youthful exuberance and innocence—He gets it because we're not judged by the letter of the law anymore. Instead, we're judged by our heart's condition.

In this case, my heart was innocent. I was wrapped up in the excitement about studying a subject I was living out, not concerned at all with what other people thought of my fast.

I still remember the way that weight lifted right off me. Yes, it was a silly little thing, but sometimes the silliest, littlest things keep us wrapped right up in fear of man, to the point where we forget that our job is to fear God alone.

Of course, God's final words on the subject were so like Him, filled with a bit of irony, *There are so many things you do need to repent of, there is no need to carry about the weight of things that are not yours.*

The glorious thing about the sins I do need forgiveness for? Even them, He condemns not. Forgiveness is freely given.

"For you did not receive a spirit that makes you a slave again to fear, but you received the Spirit of sonship. And by him we cry, 'Abba, Father '"(**Romans 8:15**).

HIS LOVE IS BETTER THAN LIFE.

JEALOUS LOVER

WordSnack: Psalm 63

I was at Bible college, surrounded by people and conversation and community, but I had never felt so alone. What was wrong with me? After growing up on a Bible school campus, I had always dreamed of the day when I would be one of the students and here I was! But something was missing.

I found the answer I needed in **Psalm 63:1**. "Oh, God, you are my God, earnestly I seek you."

The words seemed to swirl around me. I missed Him.

Oh, how silly it seemed! There at a Bible school where everything was about God, and I *missed* Him. But nothing—not fellowship, not conversation, not community—nothing can compare to the beauty of having a personal relationship with the Redeemer of all.

"My soul thirsts for you, my body longs for you, in a dry and weary land where there is no water" (**Psalm 63:1**).

For the first time in my life there were so many things, so many deadlines, so much happening, that my time with Jesus was in danger of fading into the background.

That day, as I soaked in the words from Psalms, I determined I would guard my time with my Savior like a jealous lover.

Not long ago, my daughter asked me why I close my eyes and raise my hands during worship. I smiled and brought her to this chapter. "Because, dolly," I said, pointing to the verses, "sometimes I need to just shut my eyes tight to all the things that might distract me. I need to lift my hands up to show my surrender to Jesus. To open my heart wide to His presence. To remind my soul that there is something far beyond the right-here that I am clinging to."

"Because your love is better than life, my lips will glorify you. I will praise you as long as I live, and in your name I will lift up my hands" (**Psalm 63:3-4**).

COMFORT AND STRENGTH

WordSnack: Psalm 84:5-7

I was sick for days, fighting off a nasty cold that has settled in my throat. I kept drinking gallons of hot tea with honey, and sipping cups of chicken broth, and wishing I could just sleep all day, every day.

When I'm sick, all I want are comforting things; warm blankets, soft pillows, hot tea.

Sometimes I feel like the Psalms are God's version of wrapping us tight in warmth and gentleness, right when we need it most.

That morning I read in **Psalm 84,** where the popular song, "Better is One Day" is taken from. As I read through the familiar words of the song, I came to my very favorite part.

"Blessed are those whose strength is in you," it begins. Blessing to those who are depending on Christ for their strength.

"As they go through the Valley of Baca they make it a place of springs; the early rain also covers it with pools. They go from strength to strength; each one appears before God in Zion."

The Valley of Baca was an actual place, located in desert country. A valley where there was little water and much hardship found for those passing through. The literal translation is, "Valley of Weeping" or "Valley of Tears."

God's promise, this glorious comfort that rests on us, is that those who depend on Him will travel through the valley of weeping and make the desert a place of springs. We go from strength to strength, in Him, and will leave pools of water for those coming behind us.

Is that not the most glorious of warm blankets? Comfort of all comforts.

We are held tight in His hands. Always. Even in the desert, even through the weeping, even when we are weak within ourselves.

Through Him we go from strength to strength.

IN HIM, WE GO FROM STRENGTH TO STRENGTH.

HOLD UP MY HANDS

WordSnack: Exodus 17:8-16

In **Exodus 17** we read about a nation, the Amalekites, who attacked the weakest of the Israelites as they were fleeing Egypt. At a certain point, once the people were somewhat settled into their nomad-ish new life, Moses told Joshua to take an army and meet the Amalekites in battle.

Moses, Aaron, and Hur stood and watched from a hill overlooking the battle. Whenever Moses raised his hands, with the staff of God in them, the Israelites prevailed. Whenever he lowered them, the Amalekites prevailed.

The solution seemed simple; just have Moses keep his arms up. Except, of course, any of us who have ever had to keep our arms raised for any length of time know that it is harder than it sounds.

So they found a stone for Moses to sit on and Aaron stood on one side of him and Hur stood on the other and they held Moses' arms for him.

The battle was won. God's miraculous provision was again given to His people.

It's funny, but it makes me think about marriage.

My husband and I have often laughed over the way we work through a crisis. I will be worn out and exhausted and exasperated and completely dependent on him to "hold up my hands" and offer the stability and strength I need to win whatever battle I'm facing. Then a few weeks later the positions will be switched, and I'll be holding his hands up—being the stabilizing force for him.

However, then there are days when we're both worn thin and he'll need me to hold him up and I'll think, *I can't do this! I'm too tired, too weak.* And God will speak, as He always does, and remind me that it's not really me to begin with.

Just like it wasn't really Moses or Aaron or Hur.

It's Him.

He is the stabilizing force behind all of His people. The rock we sit on, the mountain we stand on, the power that pours strength into us when we have nothing left in ourselves.

No matter what you're facing today, know this truth: *He is.*

He is God enough. He is strength enough. He is life enough. He is truth enough. He is hope enough. And He is the one who will hold you up when everything else is crumbling.

CONTENTMENT

WordSnack: 1 Timothy 6:6-12

Almost seven years were spent in the little house on the hill. People made comments sometimes, wondering that we could ever live in such a tiny place. Usually their comments only lasted as long as they were driving by and talking. Once they came inside, however, they shushed up right quick.

My husband had taken a little run-down pigeon barn and fashioned a cozy, warm homestead. Between the towering recycled dance-floor ceiling, the wall-sized windows, the golden-cherry cupboards, and the hand-crafted staircase, most people just turned around with eyes wide open when they stepped inside.

It was beautiful, and I loved every single minute we lived there.

Yes, sometimes the space was crowded. But, unlike what most people seem to think, we did not eventually move into a larger house because we wanted more space. We moved because God opened the doors for us to work at a job that would hopefully benefit our family in the long-run and would bless dear friends of ours in the meantime.

Many have commented about how we must be "so happy" to have moved. We are! But not because we felt discontent with our house.

In fact, in **1 Timothy 6** Paul says, "But godliness with contentment is great gain, for we brought nothing into the world, and we cannot take anything out of the world. But if we have food and clothing, with these we will be content."

To be honest, I'm not always good at this. I was discontent for years with our lack of children. I've been discontent with my body, my money, my possessions. But for some reason, I was always content with our home. Perhaps because it was warm and soft and the place my husband built for me with his own hands—but I think, also, because I knew, deep-down, that nothing in a home would bring me contentment if my heart was bent on discontentment.

American society says we need bigger houses, more space, better furniture, faster computers, nicer iPhones.

But God says, "Godliness with contentment is great gain."

It's normal, society will say, to work towards nicer things and prettier clothes and better vehicles.

But God says, "It is through this craving that some have wandered away from the faith and pierced themselves with many pangs."

And it was there, in that 18×24 space, with the washer and dryer in the corner of my bedroom because that's the only place it fit, and the living room that only had space for one love seat, and the kitchen that I was loathe to share because I would step on whoever wanted to help me, that I learned one of life's most important lessons. Contentment is a decision.

Contentment with my house (and the ability to see all the beautiful things about it). Contentment with my husband (and the chance to fall in love with him, day after day after day). Contentment with my family (even if it was only-ever just the two of us). Contentment with whatever God had for me—for He is always working out good for those who are called according to His purpose.

It was all a choice. One I had the chance to make every single day.

"But as for you, O man of God, flee [discontentment and the love of money]. Pursue righteousness, godliness, faith, love, steadfastness, gentleness. Fight the good fight of the faith. Take hold of the eternal life to which you were called and about which you made the good confession in the presence of many witnesses" (**1 Timothy 6:11-12**).

INSIDE OUT

WordSnack: 1 Corinthians 10:14-33

I find it interesting that, in the Scriptures, whenever we're reminded of our freedom as Believers, we are also reminded of the need for restraint. It's true that we are not under the written law any longer, but it is also true that the Holy Spirit is now writing his law on our hearts (Jeremiah 31:33).

In other words, true freedom means that we are no longer bound by outward commands, but are instead controlled by inward restraint.

Take for example, the end of **I Corinthians 10**. At face value it's talking about eating meat sacrificed to idols, something I personally do not come in contact with, well, ever. But there is so much more depth in this passage than just meat and idols.

Paul says in verse 23, "All things are lawful, but not all things are helpful. All things are lawful, but not all things build up." And then in verse 31, there is a principle we are given, the guiding boundary for all things. "So, whether you eat or drink, or whatever you do, do all to the glory of God."

If we stop and ask ourselves (honestly), *Am I doing this for God's glory?* We have found the answer to any, *Should I or shouldn't I?* question.

Yet, we can only answer for ourselves. What one person does to God's glory does not necessarily have to be duplicated in the next person.

As our friend Devin put it: "I should not try to conform others into what I think a Christian should look like. I should desire to have them share my *faith*, not necessarily my convictions. After all, if we make a rule that one mustn't break some external thing—we will never truly know what is going on internally in a brother's heart, and that's the stuff that matters."

For when we are freed from the outward restraints, we can see clearly what lies inward. And there, where truth abounds, we can all be real and be changed and allow God to transform us from the inside out.

We are being
transformed
from the
INSIDE OUT.

INFERTILITY IS JOY?

WordSnack: James 1:2-4

Once upon a time I thought infertility was destroying my faith. I didn't realize that true faith is indestructible. The part of me that was crumbling? It wasn't, nor had it ever been, faith.

James knew this truth, which is why he instructed the church in **James 1** to, "Count it all joy when you face trials of various kinds..."

Translation: *Count it joy, daughter, when you face infertility.*

If you had told me this seven years ago, I would have smiled and nodded, and then cried myself to sleep that night, because it wasn't joyful. It was horrible.

Ten years into this journey, I look back and realize he was right. What you think you believe in the sunlight may be very different than what you believe in the dark. When light is missing, that's when truth is unveiled.

In the darkness of infertility, I was forced to see truth. In the darkness of infertility, every temporary and fake thing I had was stripped away. It was just me, and a God I didn't understand.

For awhile I shunned the trials. Joy? Ha. It was hell. Yet to shun the trial is to shun being remade. Gently, this Father—with a skittish and broken daughter—carefully reached out with open arms and whispered into my deaf ears. Patiently, lovingly, He taught me to hear again, to feel.

Here's the truth: I didn't *really* know if God was my father until everything collapsed. And then, with nothing left but bitterness and God calling, I found out the difference between being a believer and being lost.

For the lost, they stand in the darkness and cry, "God, what do you think you're doing?" Yes, even the ones who claim He's not there. Because if He is, they want to blame Him.

And the true children of God? When we're done screaming, done fighting—we get to crawl, weeping, to His feet and say, *Oh, Father. Abba. Daddy. Help.*

"For you know," James continues, "the testing of your faith

produces steadfastness. And let steadfastness have its full effect, that you may be perfect and complete, lacking nothing."

Once upon a time I thought infertility was destroying my faith, but now I know that it was revealing it.

And I count it all joy.

Not pleasure. No. Not happiness. Not at all. But joy.

And this *joy* is the *settled truth that nothing is wasted when placed securely in the hands of my Father.*

This knowledge, this belief, will produce steadfastness. And the full effect of this endurance, this joy?—we will lack nothing.

Our faith will be tested, dear ones, in so many ways. We will find out what we truly believe. There is an Abba, a Father, waiting to remake us, to pour joy into us, to lead us on to completion.

DEATH SENTENCE

WordSnack: 2 Corinthians 1:8–11

There are days when we are forced to carry burdens that are larger than our strength. I know.

I still remember the day when we learned that the child we planned on adopting was no longer available to us. I was so broken, so lost, so confused. We had loved her, had shared smiles with her when she was told we would be her family. I would have done anything to keep additional pain from her, but I couldn't do a blooming thing to stop it. I nearly crumbled under the weight of the sorrow.

It was a death sentence I couldn't fight.

Paul understood this. He writes in **2 Corinthians 1** that when he and Timothy were in Asia, they had felt they were "utterly burdened beyond our strength that we despaired of life itself." But then he shared something startlingly glorious. "Indeed," he said, "we felt that we had received the sentence of death. But that was to make us rely not on ourselves but on God who raises the dead."

In the months that followed our failed adoption, I began to understand. This type of death sentence was necessary in my life. It was necessary to remind me that I cannot rely on my own strength. Ever. I have to rely on the One who is able to breath life into things that are dead.

Nine months later (oh, the beautiful little things our God does!) we brought our daughter home. No, it wasn't the child we thought God was giving us. It was the one who did not come through our will or our strength, but instead through our God who knows the beginning and the end. The One who raises the dead, and breathes life into dreams that have turned to dust.

The death sentence you are facing today? May it remind you to not rely on yourself, but on Him who raises the dead.

THOUGH I MAY NEVER BEAR A CHILD

WordSnack: Habakkuk 3:17–19

I didn't really think of the ramifications of adopting a daughter who could read well. The other day I walked into the room and she was snuggled up on the couch with *Pain Redeemed* in her hands.

Later she came to me and hugged me from behind. "Oh, Mommy," she said into my back. "I didn't know you lost a baby."

She was snuffling and wiping tears before I could react and we both ended up sitting on the kitchen floor talking about how God gives and takes away and it's okay.

"You must be so sad all the time!" she said.

"No, no," I scrambled to explain. "I'm not so sad all the time. God has been good to us."

In **Habakkuk 3:17**, the prophet is talking about all the things that may go wrong. "Though the fig tree should not blossom, nor fruit be on the vine, the produce of the olive fail and the fields yield no food..."

And I thought of all the things I could add to the list. "Though I may never bear a child, nor cradle my own infant in my arms, should I fail to have the privilege of choosing a name for a son or daughter, or watching them learn to walk and talk and laugh..."

I looked over at my beautiful girl, this precious, incredible gift that God has poured into our lives—the child I didn't get to name, or carry, or watch grow from infancy, and I say with Habakkuk, "Yet, I will rejoice in the Lord; I will take joy in the God of my salvation. God, the Lord, is my strength; he makes my feet like the deer's; he makes me tread on my high places."

No, I am not so sad. I have been sad. I have mourned deeply. But I rejoice. I rejoice in God's gracious goodness, His hand of mercy in the midst of my pain, and His brilliant promise of salvation.

GOD ALONE

puts the boundary lines in place.

FRAYED EDGES

WordSnack: Psalm 16:5-6

We were driving to church and my husband said, "I feel like I'm frayed at the edges, and any second I could unravel."

I'm wiping away tears as I nod. Yes, this is life. You walk and follow and sometimes God leads down some pretty dark and wandering roads.

Next we're at church, so late it's horrible, and I'm trying to catch up with what the speaker is sharing. I understand that he was in a plane wreck, it was a miracle he survived, he has a passion for sharing the gospel. Then he said words that stilled me.

"Remember, the verse in **Psalm 16**?" he asked us. And I started searching, and sat and stared at the page in front of me.

It's talking about God being our refuge, our safe place. It says, "Yahweh is my inheritance and my cup. You are the one who determines my destiny. Your boundary lines mark out pleasant places for me. Indeed, my inheritance is something beautiful" (**Psalm 16:5-6** GW).

This man I've never met, whose name I never caught, he speaks Holy-Spirit-led-words right there. "Looking back at my accident, all I went through, I realize that God is the one who marked out the boundary lines of what could happen, and they were in pleasant places for me. In your life, He is the one marking the boundaries."

God is my refuge. No matter how frayed along the edges I am—He is the one that marks out the boundary lines of what can happen in my life. *And He is trustworthy.*

The Hebrew word translated "pleasant" also can mean "delightful." Not perfect or wonderful or pain-free, but something that brings delight in the end. Yahweh is our inheritance, the One who determines our destiny, and the boundary lines are already in place.

Oh, thank you, Father.

WALKING BLIND

WordSnack: Isaiah 42:10-16

There are days when nothing you've ever learned in the past can tell you what to do in the moment. It's like you're facing a new road, blindfolded.

When I was eighteen, my grandparents planned to move to Florida to live with my parents. During their last visit before the move, Grandma was talking to me in the living room. We were looking at my growing collection of Grace Livingston Hill books. This was one special thing we shared, our love for these old fashioned stories.

"You know why I really love them?" Grandma said. "They are relaxing stories, where everything works out, but they still remind me of truth. Like right here."

She reached up and pulled down a book, flipped through it and pointed to a section. "These verses, they are just what I need right now. We're planning to leave the place I grew up, raised my family. We're moving to a new state, and it's all a dark road. I don't know how to navigate it, but God promises to lead us, to make the rough places smooth."

She reads, "And I will lead the blind in a way that they do not know, in paths that they have not known I will guide them. I will turn the darkness before them into light, the rough places into level ground. These are the things I do, and I do not forsake them" **(Isaiah 42:16)**.

I went into my room after our conversation and found the verses in my Bible, right there in **Isaiah 42**, and underlined them.

So many times I find myself walking a road I don't know. Wandering down paths I can't see the end of. Believing the God I serve will make the rough places smooth, that He will hold my hand and lead me around every corner and curve, every phone call, every decision, every hope. Clinging tight to the belief that the darkness will turn to light before me, as I take each step.

He is faithful. He will not forsake me. Nor will He forsake you.

He will not

FORSAKE YOU.

THE KEY TO SURVIVING HARDSHIP

WordSnack: Job 38:1-7

I think I learned to love Job the most when I was battling depression. I struggled with the conversation between Job and his friends, but then I would sit and read God's answers over and over. His glory hushed the scream of my pain. His power quieted the spinning thoughts in my head.

I read them again today, in **Job 38**. All those words God spoke from the whirlwind. *Oh, glory.*

The key to surviving hardship is found in maintaining the conversation with God. Human tendency is to pick one of three responses when facing sorrow: "God must not exist," and then shut down communication because He's not there. "God isn't really good," and then shut down communication because who wants to talk to a God who isn't good? Or "God exists, is probably good, but He doesn't really care about me personally," and shut down communication because we're not important enough.

The book of Job gives us another option. We see what happens when mere man continues his dialogue with the holy God, right past the place where he doesn't understand, right into the questions and the anger and the tears and the desperation. Right through depression and so much loss it aches to even think of it.

Here we learn that the Creator of the universe honors the man who keeps the lines of communication open. He honors him by responding, by teaching, by rebuking, by building up and pouring into.

Don't let the enemy steal your conversation with God.

The Creator is big enough for your questions. He is love enough to show up.

So keep the doors open. Keep your ears tuned to His voice. Keep your heart humble before Him. Ask, seek, and knock. He is there.

ASK, SEEK, KNOCK.
He is there.

IF I CAN'T RAISE CHILDREN

WordSnack: Isaiah 58:11-12

She was infertile, like me. Yet, somehow, some way, God opened her womb and she bore children. Then they said no more. Impossible.

The last baby, he wasn't suppose to be. The doctors said no, so we feared something was wrong, but it wasn't cancer or questions, it was another son.

When we got the call, I sat down and cried. Great heaving sobs. Joy unspeakable. I scrawled into my journal, "It's almost like something deep inside me sighed and said, *Oh, yes, God IS good. I knew it, but I doubted. I've tried so hard not to, but I did.*"

Something settled hard into me that day. I looked around with clearer sight. I saw things for what they were, instead of what the enemy was whispering.

I read **Isaiah 58**, where God promises to those who leave behind their fake religion and petty beliefs for true fasting, true belief, He will make them like a well-watered garden, like a spring whose waters never fail. They will be called Repairer of Broken Walls and Restorer of Streets with Dwelling. Names that whisper the hope of *life.*

I taped the verses from **Isaiah 58** to my windowsill, and wrote down the list of my heart.

- If I can't raise children then God must have more for me. So I will trust.
- If I can't raise children then I will be a repairer of broken walls in other people's lives.
- If I can't raise children then I will bless and encourage those God places in my path.
- If I can't raise children then I will love, with a mother's love, every child I meet.
- If I can't raise children then I will pray restoration into the lives of each person I am around.

I stopped fasting and praying for the fulfillment of my desires, and instead began praying for the grace to fulfill my list. "Like a well-watered garden," the verses said, "like a spring whose waters never fail." I tasted the wetness in my heart, the living water bubbling. *Repairer of Broken Walls,* the names filled me up, *Restorer of Streets with Dwellings.*

Today, as I read the journal entries, the verses in my Bible—underlined and highlighted, circled and dated—I breathe deep. God is good. Always, always good.

For each of us, He marks out a path. A road to travel. And He walks beside us, every step of the way. Breathing miracles into our physical lives, and more often, into our hearts. Watering the soil with His grace, His mercy, His hope, His love.

I pray that instead of being known as "barren" I might be known as Restorer and Repairer. The one who speaks Truth into the lies the enemy is whispering.

The lies about needing marriage to be fulfilled. The lies about needing children to have worth. The lies about needing a certain income, or certain clothes, or certain jobs, or certain positions.

Take your pen, friends, and write.

- If I can't get married then…
- If I can't have children then…
- If I can't work this job then…
- If I can't be this then…

What will you choose to be if your desires aren't met? Will you be a Repairer? A Restorer? Or will you sit still and listen to the enemy feeding you lies about your worth?

DOES GOD LOVE SOME MORE THAN OTHERS?

WordSnack: Acts 12:1-17

It's there in **Acts 12**. The fledgling church is empowered through the Holy Spirit, the men who once disappeared in fear during the crucifixion now step boldly into the streets. Some are killed, but the preaching goes on. The Word of Life is spreading like wildfire through the city.

James Zebedee (the brother of John) is one of them, a disciple of Jesus who once hid in fear, but he's now proclaiming the Messiah has come and will return. In anger, Herod has him arrested and put to death with the sword. Another martyr's blood is spilled.

Near the same time, Peter is seized and placed in prison. He is chained, and placed between two guards in a locked jail cell. Herod is planning another death, desiring to kill off Christians to please the Jews.

This time God moves. An angel of the Lord walks right into the jail cell, the chains fall off, Peter is told to stand up and follow. Doors open in front of them. Guards are blinded to them.

When Peter arrives at the home of Mary, mother of John-Mark, instead of letting him in, the servant girl, Rhoda, leaves him standing there and runs to exclaim to the gathered Believers, "Peter is at the door!"

They thought she was crazy, but time proves her words. It is Peter, rescued from the edge of death.

Here's the question this passage begs, *Did God love Peter more than James?*

For one, He allowed a sword to stop the beat of his heart, for another, He sent an angel to open doors and break through chains and blind soldiers. For one there seems to be no miracle at all, and for another the miracles just keep spilling.

I realize, it's the same question I struggle with daily. *Does God love the woman who bears children more than He loves me?*

Have you ever been there?

Does God love the girl who finds a husband more than the one who is single? Does God love the girl with the good marriage more than the one who struggles in hers? Does God love those who have steady income more than those who are forced to scrimp and save? Does God love the one whose illness is miraculously healed more than the one who stumbles through debilitating pain?

In verse 17, there is something that makes me pause. "But motioning to them with his hand to be silent, [Peter] described to them how the Lord had brought him out of the prison. And he said, 'Tell these things to James and to the brothers.'"

Tell these things.

This is what Peter says. To *tell* these things, and I don't think he means they're suppose to talk about how great Peter is, or how much he is loved. I think he means, *Tell everyone how God has miraculously shown His glory to us!*

When I start questioning who God loves more, I'm asking the wrong thing. It's like burying my head in dirt while the sunset is painting the skies.

Instead of saying, "Hey, God, do love *her* more than *me*?" I should be saying, *Oh, Abba, show me Your glory.*

Instead of moaning over the miracles I haven't been given, I should be shouting with joy that God does miraculous things!

None of us deserve a miracle. Peter did not deserve one more than James. I don't deserve one more than my neighbor. But sometimes, *oh, heart,* sometimes the God of the universe displays His glory in brilliant ways, and we are allowed to be witnesses of His grace.

It doesn't matter if the setting sun paints glory on your lawn, child. What matters is that the setting sun paints. No matter where we are in the world, or in our lives, if we choose to look at the sky, we'll see the swirls of colors.

And no matter where you are in the world, or in your life, if you choose to look for His glory, you'll find Him.

ABOUT THE AUTHOR

After years of infertility, Natasha and her husband welcomed home their daughter— not through birth, but through the miracle of adoption. She continues to write at NatashaMetzler.com where she explores how God takes the brokenness of life and pairs it up with the glory of redemption.

AN EXCERPT FROM

PAIN REDEEMED: WHEN OUR DEEPEST SORROWS MEET GOD

There are hundreds of ways that pain can rip through our lives.

How are we to face it?
How do we keep from crumbling under the weight?

Pain Redeemed takes you on a journey through my walk of infertility and with honesty and raw truthfulness tells the story of God meeting me there, right in the middle.

Are you wondering where He is?

Come taste the miracle of Pain Redeemed.

Those days were long and dark. Days that blended into months.

Over and over I found myself in tears. I would lecture my emotions and fight my sorrow but I would still end up beaten and bruised and heartbroken.

Infertility is a silent monster that slowly steals joy until there is nothing left. I can't tell you how long I hid the truth from myself but I know that time passed and I stood empty.

In the book of Isaiah, God says,

> *Why should you be beaten anymore?...your whole head is injured, your whole heart afflicted. From the sole of your foot to the top of your head there is no soundness—only wounds and welts and open sores, not cleansed or bandaged nor soothed with oil. (1:5-6)*

I was clinging to my bitter pain and God was calling me. He had not forgotten. He was pleading with me, *Why, Tasha, why? Why are you staying in this place of torture? You're wounded. Let me care for you...*

He wanted to cleanse my sorrows. He wanted to bandage my brokenness. He was begging and I was so blind and deaf that I chose to stumble in darkness instead of dancing in light.

God didn't leave me there. He called me out. I still remember the day that I read those verses in Isaiah and realized they were written for me. God, in His graciousness, pulled me up and set my feet on firm ground.

I've been listening to a lot of women. Hurting, broken women. They look alive and well but inside there are wounds and welts and open sores. I hear their stories and see the flicker of pain in their eyes. They live in darkness too.

I know that place. I've lived there. I came out of there. And I still slide back there far too often. I long for us all to find a way to live in the light. The brilliant, life-giving light.

This book is a story about sorrow but it is also about God. It's a story about me but it also about you.

Your pain may be different than mine. There are hundreds of ways that heartache can rip through our lives. The kind of pain doesn't change the truth. *God is the same no matter what type of agony we face.*

PAIN REDEEMED CAN BE FOUND AT
NATASHAMETZLER.COM/PAIN-REDEEMED
AND AMAZON.COM

82134813R00052

Made in the USA
Columbia, SC
29 November 2017